What Preteens Want Their Parents to Know

Ryan Holladay and Friends

McCRACKEN PRESS

New York

McCracken Press™

An imprint of Multi Media Communicators, Inc.

575 Madison Avenue, Suite 1006
New York, NY 10022

McCracken Press™ is a trademark of Multi Media Communicators, Inc.

Cover by Jim Hellman

Library of Congress Cataloging-in-Publication Data:
Holladay, Ryan.
    What preteens want their parents to know / Ryan Holladay and friends.—1st ed.
       p.   cm.
    ISBN 1-56977-475-7 ; $5.95
      1. Preteens—United States—Miscellanea. 2. Parent and child—United States—Miscellanea. I. Title.
HQ777.15.H65 1994   94-8329
306.874—dc20   CIP

10 9 8 7 6 5 4 3 2
First Edition
Printed in the United States of America

This book is dedicated to my parents.

Introduction

You parents are funny. Even though you were once preteens yourselves, it seems that most of you have forgotten that period of your life. At least it seems that way to me and to most of my friends.

I can see why many of you don't want to remember this time. It's really a weird one—going from being a little kid to a teenager. It is a time of change and challenge—physically, emotionally, socially.

Yet even though this is a tough time for us all, we need your support, your friendship, your guidance, and most of all, your love.

And so, with a little help from my friends, I decided to write this book. You already know some of these things, but sometimes you forget. This is an important time for us. We only travel this road together once. Let's make the most of it.

Ryan Holladay
Washington, D.C.

What Preteens Want
Their Parents to Know

Encourage me when I do a good job.

—

Let me teach *you* some things. Don't always be the teacher.

Don't show too much affection in public.

—

Let me take some risks; you did when you were young.

Try not to miss my ball games, school plays, or the other activities that are special to me.

Respect my privacy.

Say "yes" more often than "no."

—

Take me on short errands with
you if I want to go.

Getting a pet is a great idea.

—

Set limits on the amount of television
I watch.

Help me to develop a skill or talent
that will last a lifetime.

—

Give me reasons for your demands.

Family activities really make
me feel close to everyone.

Take time to explain things to me.

—

Don't take it personally when I act
weird . . . sometimes I feel weird.

Hang out with me sometimes.

—

Understand that I don't try to make you
mad; it just happens. I don't like being
on your bad side.

Please stop showing pictures of me to everyone you meet. This is very embarrassing.

Tell me what's going on with family problems or any other problems. It hurts me when I know that I'm not being included.

Board games can be
fun to play with the family.

—

Tell me about your first date.

Keep your word.

Keep praying for me.
It makes me feel secure.

Ask forgiveness of me sometimes.

—

Don't let me sleep *too* late in the
summer. I might miss something
that I really wanted to do.

25

Don't always give me what I keep
asking you for.

—

Make sure you listen to my answers
when you ask me questions.

Listening is one of the best ways to show me you love me.

If I spend a lot of time
on the phone with my friends,
don't get worked up.

Stop comparing me to my brothers or sisters or to my classmates. We are all different and want to be treated as individuals.

If I lose at something, let me have some time to myself. Later you can tell me what I did wrong...and what I did right.

Always buy me clothes that are in fashion, not something you would wear.

—

Spread your love around. Give equal attention to each child in the family.

I enjoy seeing my parents hug.

Don't make fun of the music I listen to
or the clothes I wear.

—

Set high moral standards for me.

Never buy me underwear that could
embarrass me in gym class.

—

Wear your seat belt.
You're important to me.

Keep telling me you love me
and are proud of me.

Teach me how to act around adults.

—

Never put me down, especially in front
of my friends.

Talk to me about all subjects, even sensitive ones like AIDS, dating, etc. I need information.

Encourage me to earn
my own money.

Keep pushing me to learn how to express myself in words, both written and spoken. It really does help me to think better.

Pray with me.

—

Teach me about different religions,
cultures, and races.

Get to know my friends. Include
them in some of our family plans.

—

Discuss movies after we see them.
This teaches me to evaluate things.

Don't tell me my fears are silly.

—

Let me express myself through
my hair and clothes.

Even though I complain
about music lessons, make me
stick with them.

Keep encouraging me to follow *my* dreams. Mine are different than yours.

—

Encourage me to save and not to buy things so quickly.

Encourage me to be honest.

—

Don't keep changing the rules.

Make sure I have a
quiet place and a regular
time to do homework.

Trust me.

Nagging doesn't work in the long run.

—

I can't always get good grades—sometimes I get nervous and make mistakes.

Don't push me into a specific sport.
Introduce me to lots of activities and
let me choose what I like.

Teach me to be kind.

—

Don't correct my mistakes in front of my
friends. Save your criticisms until we're
alone.

Arguments are a natural part of
being a family.

—

Don't begin sentences with "When
I was your age..."

Let me be independent and learn to
govern myself. I'll do the driving;
you do the navigating.

Have at least one meal as a family each day.

Ask open-ended questions, it helps me
solve my own problems.

—

Tell me about our family history, it
makes me proud.

Set clear, consistent boundaries.

—

Share the experiences that you
had as a kid—even the mistakes and
embarrassing times.

Tell me when you're in a bad mood or are having a bad day. That way I won't be so hurt if you say something dumb.

I like us to go to church
together as a family.

—

Set a good example for me when it
comes to habits like drinking. Do these
things in moderation, if at all.

Remember I can't read
your mind.

Teach me to keep trying.

I need rules, but not too many.

—

When I'm with my friends, don't always try to hang out with us. You and I can spend time together later.

Let me help decide on my own bedtime.

—

Occasionally I still like to be kissed by
both of my parents.

Cheer for my whole team,
not just for me.

—

Know what I'm watching on TV. I am
really not old enough to see some things.

Your praise
means more to me
than anyone else's.

Make sure that my friends feel welcome at our house.

73

Don't say things you don't mean
when you are angry.

—

Sometimes discuss problems with me
when you don't know the solutions.

Instead of giving orders, offer choices.

—

Never, never call me by a pet
name in public.

Give me more responsibilities
as I prove myself ready.

—

Let me decorate my own room, but you
can give me advice.

Encourage me to start a collection of something interesting.

Teach me good manners.

—

Rent videos with a message for
the family to watch.

Be aware of the music I listen to. Take the time to introduce me to other types of music.

Teach me to compare prices
before buying.

Read the newspaper with me sometimes
and discuss what's going on.

—

Let me go to the movies with a friend.
We'll get the tickets and the food and
meet you later.

Always make time for me.
We can sit around and talk,
read a book, or do something else.
The important thing is that you like to
spend time with me.

Help me to pick out
good books.

Don't make any promises you might
not be able to keep.

—

Take me with you to work. It helps me
to understand who you are.

Occasionally watch my favorite TV shows with me.

—

I like it when you have fun with my friends and me. They usually don't see parents acting so crazy.

Don't bottle up your problems.
Share them.

—

Think of recreational things we
can do together.

Pets teach responsibility.

Whenever possible, let us kids resolve our differences by ourselves. We need to learn to work things out for ourselves. We can't always rely on you to be around to solve every problem.

Compliment my friends.

—

Tell me about your disappointments.

Don't spend all your time on the child who's acting up. Acknowledge the good as well as the bad.

Don't be sarcastic.

Teach me right and wrong.

—

Allow me to use some of your valuable
possessions like your camcorder and
camera.

Help me to learn some world geography.
I need to understand other people,
other places.

Teach me how to cook.

Let me see you helping someone in need.

—

Sometimes listen to my friends and me
talking without adding your
own opinion.

Show me how to compete.

—

Let's once in a while take turns
reading out loud.

Keep a chart of my accomplishments.

—

Try not to embarrass me by the way
you dress.

Let me choose my own friends.

—

Answer my questions, even the ones about sex.

Teach me to be a good winner and a good loser.

—

Please don't yell at me when there's a problem. The less anger the easier it is to understand one another.

The next time I have a day off from school, take a day off from work and spend the time with me. You can get to know me better.

When telling me about your rules, make sure I understand the consequences.

—

Even smart kids are going to make mistakes. I'm smart, not perfect.

Don't keep adding on punishments.
Don't ground me and then decide that
I also can't use the phone, and then that
I also can't watch TV.

Keep encouraging me
to read.

Remember that my room is the only
private place I can call my own. If
I don't want to keep it perfectly neat,
let me.

Make up a list of my chores. That way I know exactly what I need to do and you won't have to keep reminding me.

Don't just teach me about sex; teach me about love.

—

Help me plan ahead. High school will be scary enough even *with* a plan.

Try to remember what it was like being my age.

Introduce me to lots of different things. Even if I never want to do something again, you have given me the experience.

Relax.

Teach me to pray about my problems.

—

Give me enough allowance so that I can
learn how to spend wisely and
how to save.

If you must fight, remember that I'm close enough to hear you.

—

Don't be so overprotective. If I'm not allowed to make mistakes, I can't learn from my mistakes.

Don't judge my friends by their clothes or hair. After all, I saw something in them that made me want their friendship.

I like the little private notes you
sometimes leave me.

Help me with my homework
when I need you to.

If I come home late,
I might have a good reason.
Ask for it before you get upset.

Teach me to be kind.

—

Don't punish me
if I don't do well in school. Instead, work
with me to improve.

I'm no longer the
little child you think of me as, but I'm
also not as grown-up as I like to pretend.

Talk to me about God.

Encourage me to use a computer.
I'll be glad later.

—

When I ask a question, make sure
I understand your answer.

Give me my allowance monthly rather than weekly. This will allow me to buy better quality things.

Don't bring up past mistakes.
Forgive and forget.

Don't automatically blame until you know the facts.

—

Take me to the hospital sometimes when you visit friends who are ill. It makes me appreciative of good health.

Believe in me.

Help me to get organized.

—

Assist with my chores when
I ask for help.

Listen to my music with me occasionally.

Teach me to respect adults.

A clothes allowance teaches me to make
good choices and saves us all hassles.

—

When I have a bad attitude or do
something mean, tell me.

Never let me smoke.

Pay my allowance on a regular basis.
Don't make me have to ask for it.

—

Listen to my jokes.

Don't assume my teen years will be a hassle. You might actually enjoy me as a teenager.

Have a set time for us to do family chores.

—

I like it when you play practical jokes on us.

Look at family photo albums with me
and tell me about the relatives.

Don't always let me win when
we play games or sports.

Don't shout to make a point.

Never call anybody
stupid or dumb.

Encourage me to exercise
regularly.

Even when I do something wrong, let
me know you love me.

—

Don't set unrealistic goals.

Sometimes I just want
to be left alone.

Control the amount of time
I play video games.

—

Don't get too concerned if I occasionally
use bathroom humor.

I like it when you have fun
with me.

Thank me and point it out
when I'm polite.

—

Allow me to keep some of my money
in a safe, secret place.

Make sure that I understand the meaning behind the words on my posters and T-shirts.

Ask my advice sometimes.

—

Let yourself be a parent,
not a policeman.

Remember that even though
I don't always say it,
I appreciate all you do for me.

I'd like to add...

_____

_____

_____

_____

I'd like to add . . .

_____

_____

_____

_____

I'd like to add . . .

_____

_____

_____

_____

I'd like to add . . .

_____

_____

_____

_____

Note from the Author

I would like to thank all those who contributed to this book, including Jody Brown, Josh Chetta, Michael Cody, Bret Farris, C. J. Guinness, Hilary Hinsey, Hays Holladay, Colin Holmes, Samantha Holmes, Gail Martin, Deanna Ruhl, and Melissa Scalzi.

Ryan Holladay is 12 years old and resides with his parents and two younger brothers in Washington, D.C. He attends Rivendell School and is currently pursuing an acting career.

If you would like to contribute to books in this series, please send your ideas to:

Ryan Holladay
McCracken Press
575 Madison Avenue, Suite 1006
New York, NY 10022